CW00666611

Western Main Lines

PLYMOUTH TO ST. AUSTELL

Vic Mitchell and Keith Smith

MP Middleton Press

Cover picture: Ancient and modern bridges flank a member of the now obsolete class 50. No. 50023 **Howe** *enters Cornwall with the 13.40 from Paddington on 20th July 1984. The sign was erected by Cornish Railways, a short lived local initiative soon swept away by the "Railway Meddlers of Westminster". (G.Gillham)*

Published March 2001

ISBN 1 901706 63 X

© Middleton Press, 2001

Design	*Deborah Esher*
Typesetting	*Barbara Mitchell*

Published by
> *Middleton Press*
> *Easebourne Lane*
> *Midhurst, West Sussex*
> *GU29 9AZ*

Tel: 01730 813169
Fax: 01730 812601

Printed & bound by Biddles Ltd,
> *Guildford and Kings Lynn*

CONTENTS

ACKNOWLEDGEMENTS

We are very grateful for the help received from so many of the photographers. Our thanks also go to N.L.Browne, D.B.Clayton, H.Cowan, G.Croughton, A.Dasi-Sutton, F.Hornby, N.Langridge, L.W.Rowe, Mr D. and Dr S.Salter, G.T.V.Stacey, E.Youldon and our ever supportive wives.

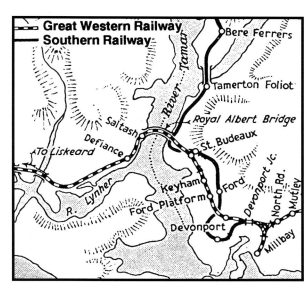

I.   The Plymouth area lines are shown in 1923. (Railway Magazine)

II.   Railway Clearing House map of the freight and passenger lines in 1923. The SR lines are solid and the GWR lines are hollow.

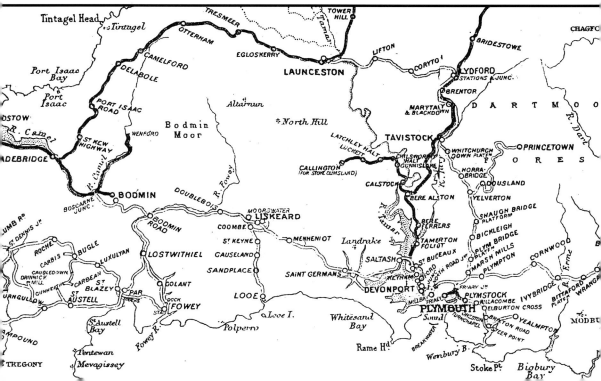

GEOGRAPHICAL SETTING

The deep valley of the River Tamar has acted as a significant barrier separating Devon and Cornwall, the early railway promoters planning a train ferry for its crossing. Its sheltered estuary at its confluence with the River Plym in Plymouth Sound formed a natural harbour in which Naval and merchant shipping activities developed greatly. The former took place largely on the west flank of Plymouth, while commercial docks developed on the southern shoreline.

The railways grew to serve both these areas and the Tamar was eventually crossed on the lofty Royal Albert Bridge and Cornwall was entered at Saltash. The line initially ran west close to the Lynher River, but was later realigned further north to cross it more than a mile east of St. Germans. There were originally 26 viaducts between Plymouth and St. Austell, but the diversion reduced the number by two.

An undulating course is followed over a deeply incised landscape, the line crossing the River Seaton near Menheniot station and the East Looe River west of Liskeard. It enters the deep valley of the River Fowey near Doublebois and descends in it for about ten miles to Lostwithiel.

A climb over a headland includes Treverrin Tunnel and a steep descent to Par, where the busy harbour is skirted. The climb to St. Austell is roughly parallel to the coast. The town is the centre of the china clay industry, which generated traffic at several locations near the route. However, most of the line was laid on Red Sandstone of limited economic value.

The maps are to the scale of 25ins to 1 mile, unless shown otherwise.

III.   Gradient profile

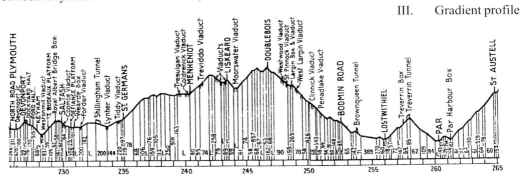

HISTORICAL BACKGROUND

The Act for the Cornwall Railway to build a single track broad gauge line from Plymouth to Falmouth was passed on 3rd August 1846. It was financed jointly by three other railways - the Bristol & Exeter, the Great Western and the South Devon. The consulting engineer was Mr I.K.Brunel who proposed bridging the River Tamar instead of using a train ferry, as originally planned.

The SDR had reached Plymouth (Laira Green) on 5th May 1848 and the broad gauge line was extended to Millbay on 2nd April 1849.

London & South Western Railway trains began running into Plymouth on 17th May 1876.

They went via Okehampton to Lydford from where they traversed the GWR branch, travelling through Tavistock, Marsh Mills and Laira to reach the LSWR terminus at Devonport. North Road station did not open until 28th March 1877.

The Plymouth, Devonport & South Western Junction Railway constructed a line between Devonport and Lydford, this being the route for all LSWR trains from 2nd June 1890. It passed under the Cornwall line twice near the east bank of the Tamar at St. Budeaux.

The route between Plymouth Millbay and Truro opened to passengers on 2nd May 1859 and to freight in the following October.

At Liskeard the line passed over the Liskeard & Caradon Railway, which carried passengers between Moorswater and Looe from 1879. The connection to Liskeard was made in 1901.

The branch from Bodmin Road (now Parkway) to Bodmin was in use from 1887 to 1967 for passengers, but some freight continued until 1983. A steam service was reintroduced in 1990.

From Lostwithiel there is a mineral branch to Fowey, which opened in 1869 and carried passengers between 1895 and 1965, except during wartime.

Near Par the route passed over the Cornwall Minerals Railway, which was opened between Fowey and Newquay on 1st June 1874. It carried passengers from 1876 and was of standard gauge. The Par-St.Blazey connection opened in 1879.

The main line trains were operated by the GWR from 1st October 1877, the CR and SDR having been linked directly in Plymouth in the previous year. The GWR took over the CR in 1889 and the conversion to standard gauge followed on 20-21 May 1892.

The doubling of the track took place in stages thus:

Cornwall Junction to Devonport	1860
Devonport to Royal Albert Bridge	October 1899 to July 1903
Saltash to Wearde Siding	February 1906
Wearde Siding to St. Germans	May 1908
St. Germans to Tresulgan Viaduct	December 1897
Tresulgan Viaduct to Trevido	May 1896 to June 1899
Trevido Viaduct to Liskeard	August 1896
Liskeard to Doublebois	February 1894
Doublebois to Bodmin Road	December 1893
Bodmin Road to Lostwithiel	July 1893
Lostwithiel to Par	October 1895
Par to St. Austell	October 1893

Passenger services ceased at Plymouth Millbay on 23rd April 1941, but traffic continued to Plymouth Docks until 30th June 1971.

The area passed to the Western Region of British Railways upon nationalisation in 1948. The effects of privatisation in the mid-1990s resulted in passenger services being operated by Great Western Trains, Virgin Cross Country and Wales & West. South West Trains ran one trip per week from September 2000.

PASSENGER SERVICES

Plymouth - St. Austell

The metal mining boom was in decline when the line opened and so a minimal service was provided. Tourism was a long way off, but gradually the railway responded and helped its development.

During the 19th century almost all trains from London reversed at Plymouth at the Millbay terminus, but by 1902 there were two on weekdays that ran direct, using the northern part of the triangular junction provided for LSWR trains. In 1920, seven out of eight trains used this route and in 1938 the figures were 12 out of 14, the others commencing at Millbay.

A summary of down train frequencies is given, the figures in brackets being trains terminating at Liskeard. In many years, there were one or two trains running as far as St. Germans or Menheniot.

	Weekdays	Sundays
1869	4 (1)	2 (1)
1885	7 (1)	3
1902	10 (3)	3
1920	8 (2)	3
1938	14 (2)	6 (1)
1950	13 (3)	4 (1)
1968	12	5
1986	17	9

Extra trains for holiday makers on Summer Saturdays began to appear in the 1920s and, after a wartime break, reached their zenith in the 1950s.

Named trains have for long been a feature of the route. "The Cornish Riviera" was introduced in 1904 and was one of the few to be retained during World War II. "The Cornishman" ran from London from 1890 to about 1914 and from Birmngham via Stratford-upon-Avon from 1952 until 1962. "The Royal Duchy" first worked from London in 1957.

Plymouth - Saltash

In response to the growth of Saltash as a residential area, the GWR provided a local service and the number of trains from Plymouth terminating there are shown. The figures include those that ran on to Defiance Platform; 18 in 1930 for example. These short workings to Saltash were discontinued in May 1972, due to the presence of the new road bridge.

	Weekdays	Sundays
1902	4	2
1904	11	8
1917	32	7
1930	40	17
1942	22	13
1950	23	15
1960	27	16
1965	16	0
1967	6	0

The 1904 railmotor service was a great success and was soon increased to the frequency shown in this October 1905 timetable. Note that many did not call at North Road.

RAIL MOTOR CARS—One Class only.
PLYMPTON, PLYMOUTH (Millbay), KEYHAM, and SALTASH.—Great Western.

The 1966-67 weekday timetable includes trains to Gunnislake, these being shown as calling at St. Budeaux Victoria Road Halt. The note "a" indicates trains terminating at Saltash. All trains calling at St. Germans and Menheniot terminated at Liskeard, except those arriving at 08.11, 16.23 and 18.38. The timetable is continued opposite.

PLYMPTON, PLYMOUTH, and SALTASH

Week Days

Miles		a.m	a.m	a.m	a.m	a.m	a.m	a.m	a.m	a.m	a.m	a.m	a.m	a.m	a.m	a.m	a.m	a.m	a.m	a.m	a.m
		3		3		E	S		3			8 0		8 40		3		9 34	E	D	Z	E
—	Plympton ...... dep	..	..	..	..	..	..	..	8 0	..	8 40	..	..	..	9 34					
—	Marsh Mills .... dep	..	..	..	..	720	..	835	..	..	..	919	..	..	1138
4	Plymouth { arr	..	..	..	..	733	8 7	847	8 43	8 55	915	9 25	926	9 43	1147
	(North Road) { dep	5 30	6 10	6 30	6 43	6 50	7 0	7 24	7 40	8 10	8 38	8 55	915	9 25	9 50	1020	1043	1115	1157
5¼	Devonport, Albert Rd..	5 34	6 14	6 34	6 47	6 54	7 4	7 28	7 44	8 14	8 42	8 59	9 29	9 54	1024	1047	1119	12 1
5½	Dockyard Halt..........	5 36	6 16	6 36	6 49	..	7 30	..	8 16	8 44	9 1	9 56
6½	Keyham................	5 39	6 19	6 39	6 52	..	7 34	7 47	8 19	8 47	9 4	9 32	9 59	1027	1051	12 5
7	St. Budeaux, Ferry Rd..	5 42	6 22	6 42	6 55	..	7 37	..	8 22	8 50	9 7	9 35	10 2	1030	1054	12 8
8¼	Saltash............ arr	5 46	6 29	6 47	7 5	7 1	7 11	7 42	7 54	8 26	8 54	9 12	924	9 39	10 6	1035	11 0	1128	1213

Week Days—continued

		a.m	a.m	a.m	p.m	p.m	p.m	p.m	p.m	p.m	pm	p.m	p.m	p.m	p.m	p.m	p.m	p.m	pm	p.m	p.m	p.m	p.m	p.m	pm
		S	E	S	E	A		S	E	S	S	S	A	E	S	E		S	S	S	A	E	A
		3					3	1 31	3		..	216	3							3					
Plympton ...... dep		1138	..	..	..	..	1 31	..	..	216	..	..	337								
Marsh Mills .... dep		1138	..	1 13	..	..		216	..	..	337	..	..	..	5 8
Plymouth { arr		1155	..	1 22	1 40	..	225	230	..	..	350	..	..	515
(North Road) { dep		12 5	12 5	1230	1 0	1 5	1 30	1 47	2 5	2 35	3 15	3 17	3 45	4 10	4 18	4 30	4 35	4 50	5 8
Devonport, Albert Rd...		12 9	12 9	1234	1 4	1 9	1 34	1 51	2 10	2 39	3 21	3 21	3 49	4 14	4 22	4 40	4 45	5 13
Dockyard Halt..........		..	1211	..	1 11	1 26	1 53	2 41	4 24	4 56	5 15
Keyham................		1214	1214	1238	1 8	1 15	1 39	1 56	2 14	2 44	3 25	3 25	3 52	4 17	4 28	4 44	4 59	5 18
St. Budeaux, Ferry Rd..		1217	1217	1242	..	1 18	1 42	1 59	2 18	2 47	3 29	3 29	3 57	4 21	4 31	4 47	5 21
Saltash............ arr		1222	1222	1246	1 15	1 24	1 48	2 5	2 18	2 51	3 36	3 36	4 1	4 25	4 35	4 40	4 51	5 6	5 26

Week Days—continued

		p.m	p.m	p.m	p.m	p.m	p.m	pm	p.m	pm	p.m	p.m	p.m	p.m	p.m	p.m	p.m	p.m
		E	S	S	A	S	E				3	3	3	S	3	3	3	3
Plympton ...... dep		..	..	5E27	..	6 21	..	7 17	..	834	..	9 18	..	1057				
Marsh Mills .... dep		..	..	5E38	..	6 35	716	725	730	742	750	845	9 18	9 25	11 5	1057
Plymouth { arr		5 23	5 35	5E38	5 50	6 15	6 30	6 48	7 30	7 40	825	9 20	9 25	1025	11 5
(North Road) { dep		5 23	5 35	5 50	6 15	6 30	6 48	7 40	825	9 20	1025	1110	6 10	7 5	7 40	9 20	9 45	10 0
Devonport, Albert Rd...		5 26	5 39	5 46	6 19	6 34	6 52	7 44	828	9 24	1029	1114	6 14	7 10	7 44	9 24	9 50	10 4
Dockyard Halt..........		..	5 41	..	6 21	6 54	7 46	9 26	1031	1116	6 16	7 13	9 26	10 6
Keyham................		5 29	5 44	5 51	6 24	6 57	7 49	831	9 29	1034	1119	6 20	7 17	7 49	9 29
St. Budeaux, Ferry Rd..		5 32	5 47	6 0	6 27	7 0	7 52	834	9 32	1037	1122	6 23	7 20	7 50	9 32	9 55	10 9
Saltash............ arr		5 37	5 51	6 6	6 31	6 43	7 4	7 56	839	9 36	1041	1127	6 27	7 25	7 54	9 36	10 0	1014

Sundays

		a.m	a.m	a.m	a.m	a.m
		3				3
Plympton ...... dep		..	..	..	..	..
Marsh Mills .... dep		..	..	..	..	..

Sundays—continued

		a.m	a.m	p.m	p.m	p.m	p.m	p.m	p.m	p.m	p.m	pm	p.m	p.m	p.m	p.m
		3						3				3			3	
Plympton ...... dep		..	1223	..	..	..	..	..	6 5	..	7 43	..	9 38
Marsh Mills .... dep		..	..	1239	..	5 9	..	6 15	..	7 49	..	..
Plymouth { arr		..	..	1232	1247	..	5 9	..	6 15	7 55	..	9 50
(North Road) { dep		1015	1130	1255	2 15	3 25	4 5	4 50	5 40	5 55	6 50	7 3	8 10	9 0	9 20	10 0
Devonport, Albert Rd...		1019	1134	1259	2 19	3 29	4 9	4 54	5 44	5 59	6 54	7 7	8 14	9 4	9 24	10 4
Dockyard Halt..........		1021	1136	1 1	2 21	4 11	4 56	6 1	7 9	8 16	9 6	10 6
Keyham................		1024	1139	1 4	2 24	3 32	4 14	4 59	6 4	6 57	7 12	8 19	9 9	9 27	10 9
St. Budeaux, Ferry Rd..		1027	1142	1 7	2 27	3 35	4 17	5 2	6 7	7 15	8 22	9 12	9 31	1012
Saltash............ arr		1031	1146	1 11	2 31	3 39	4 21	5 6	6 12	7 5	7 19	8 26	9 16	9 36	1016

D 1st and 3rd class on Saturdays.
E or E Except Sats.
S Saturdays only.
Z Third class only on Saturdays
3 Third class only.

June 1950

			SX	SO	SO				SX	SO	SO	A					B								
PLYMOUTH ... d			11 43	12 05	12 15	12 25	12 40	13 05	13 10	13 15	13 30	13 47		14 38	15 13	15 25		15 45	16 10	16 20	16 38		16 45
DEVONPORT ALBERT ROAD ... d			..	12 09	12 19	12 29	12 44	..	13 14	13 19	13 34			..	..			15 29		15 49	16 14	16 24	16 42		16 49
DOCKYARD HALT ... d			..	12 11	12 21	12 31	12 46	..	13 16	13 21	13 36			..	..					15 51	16 16	16 26	16 45		16 51
KEYHAM ... d			..	12 13	12 23	12 33	12 48	..	13 18	13 23	13 38			..	..			15 32		15 53	16 18	16 28	16 47		16 53
ST BUDEAUX { FERRY ROAD / VICTORIA ROAD HALT... a			..	12 16	12 26	..	12 51	..	13 21		13 41			..	..			15 56		16 21	16 31	16 50		16 56
SALTASH ... d			11 53	12 20	12 30	..	12 36	12a55	13 15	13a30	13a45			14 48	15 23				16 21					
ST GERMANS ... d			..	12 28	12 38	..	..	..	..	..	..			..	..			16 00		16a35				17b03
MENHENIOT ... d			..	12 37	12 47	..	..	..	..	..	..			..	..			16 08						17 10
LISKEARD ... a			12 11	12 43	12 53	..	..	13 33	..	..	14 15			15 07	15 42			16 17				17 10		17 19
																		16 23						17 25

									SX															
PLYMOUTH ... d			16 50	17 00	17 12	17 15	..	17 33	17 40		18 00	18 10	18 15		18 55	19 10	19 15	19 55	20 53	21 30		21 35	22 30
DEVONPORT ALBERT ROAD ... d			16 54	17 04	..	17 19	..	17 37	17 44		18 04	18 14	18 19		19 14	19 19	19 59				21 39	22 34
DOCKYARD HALT ... d			16 56	17 06	..	17 21	..	17 39	17 46		18 06	18 16	18 21		19 16	19 21	20 01				21 41	22 36
KEYHAM ... d			16 58	17 08	..	17 23	..	17 41	17 48		18 08	18 18	18 23		19 18	19 23	20 03				21 43	22 38
ST BUDEAUX { FERRY ROAD / VICTORIA ROAD HALT... a			17 02	..	17 11	17 26	..	17 44	17 51		18 11		18 26		19 21		20 06	21 37				22 41
SALTASH ... d			..	17a15	17 22	..	17 48	..	18 15	18 21	18a30		19 05	19a25	20 10	21 03	21 42		21 46	22a45
ST GERMANS ... d			..	..	..	17 56	..	18 23					20 18
MENHENIOT ... d			..	..	18 05	..	18 32					20 27
LISKEARD ... a			..	17 40	..	18 11	..	18 38			19 23		20 33	21 21	22 00

A 28 May, 4 and 11 June
B 13 June to 2 September   b Arr 17 00

THROUGH TRAINS BETWEEN
GLASGOW, EXETER, PLYMOUTH, and PENZANCE.

Week Days. (Glasgow → Penzance)

Page Ref.	Station	mrn A		aft B	
	Glasgow (Central) ......dep.	10 5	..	5 30	..
	Motherwell .... "	10 27	...	..	
	Law Junction .... "	..		6 15	
732	Carstairs .... "	..		6 42	
	Symington .... "	11 8	..	6 55	
	Beattock .... "	11F30		7 32	
	Lockerbie .... "	aft		7 50	
	Carlisle .... "	12 30		8 34	
	Carnforth .... "			10 3	
428	Preston .... "	2 29		10 50	
429	Warrington (Bank Quay). "	..		11 31	
				mrn	
	Crewe .... arr.	3 30		12 1	
486	Crewe .... dep.	4 7		1 25	
487	Shrewsbury (General) .... "	5 0		2 40	
	Hereford .... arr.	6 6		3 47	
120	Pontypool Road.... "	7 0			
to	Bristol { Stapleton Road.. "	8 0			
123	Bristol { Temple Meads { arr.	8 6		6 45	
	{ dep.	9 0		6 15 6 45	
	Yatton .... arr.			.. 7 8	
12	Puxton and Worle .. "			7 17	
14a	Weston-super-Mare .. "		6 40	7 24	
15	Highbridge .... "			7 48	
	Bridgwater (G.W.) .. "	9 40		7 9 8 5	
	Durston .... "			7 24	
	Taunton .... "	9 57		7 33 8 22	
	Wellington .... "			8 45	
	Burlescombe .... "			8 55	
	Tiverton Junction .... "		8 12	9 8	
	Cullompton .... "			9 18	
	Hele and Bradninch... "			9 29	
	Exeter St. David's .. "	10 41	8 30	9 41	
	Exeter St. Thomas .. "			10 0	
	Starcross .... "			10 12	
	Dawlish Warren .... "			10 17	
12	Dawlish .... "	11 5		10 22	
25	Teignmouth .... "	11 14		10 30	
	Newton Abbot ...... "	11 23	9 8	10 39	
	Totnes .... "	11 50		11 8	
	Brent .... "			11 2)	
	Wrangaton .... "			11 32	
	Bittaford Platform .. "			11 33	
	Ivybridge .... "			11 41	
	Cornwood .... "			11 46	
	Plympton .... "			11 54	
	Plymouth { North Road.. "	mrn 12 25	10 5	12 0	
	Plymouth { Millbay .. "	12 40		12 15	
	Devonport (G.W.).... arr.			10 28	
	Saltash .... "			10 36	
	St. Germans .... "			10 45	
	Menheniot .... "			10 56	
	Liskeard .... "			11 4	
	Bodmin Road........ "			11 20	
	Lostwithiel .... "			11 27	
	Par .... "			11 38	
	St. Austell .... "			11 49	
22				aft	
	Truro .... "			12 11	
	Chacewater........ "			12 32	
	Redruth .... "			12 42	
	Camborne .... "			12 51	
	Gwinear Road ...... "			12 57	
	Hayle .... "			1 4	
	St. Erth .... "			1 9	
	Marazion .... "			1 19	
	Penzance .... "			1 25	

(B column vertical notes: "Pullman Restaurant Car, Glasgow to Carlisle." — "Week Day arrivals." — "Restaurant Car, Glasgow to Crewe." — "Sunday arrivals.")

Week Days. (Penzance → Glasgow)

Page Ref.	Station	mrn D		aft C	
	Penzance ....dep.			12 10	
	Marazion .... "			12 16	
	St. Erth .... "			12 21	
	Hayle .... "			12 32	
	Gwinear Road ...... "			12 45	
	Camborne .... "			12 52	
	Redruth .... "			1 2	
	Chacewater .... "			1 12	
	Truro .... "			1 28	
29	St. Austell .... "			1 58	
	Par .... "			2 11	
	Lostwithiel .... "			2 23	
	Bodmin Road ...... "			2 34	
	Doublebois .... "			2 48	
	Liskeard .... "			2 56	
	Menheniot .... "				
	St. Germans .... "			3 12	
	Saltash .... "			3 23	
	Devonport (G.W.).. "			3 35	
	Plymouth { Millbay ...dep.	8 45		3 55	
	Plymouth { North Road.. "	8 52			
	Totnes .... "	9 23			
	Paignton ....dep.				
	Torquay .... "				
27	Torre .... "				
29	Newton Abbot ...... arr.				
	Newton Abbot ......dep.	9 48		4 49	
	Teignmouth .... "	10 0			
	Dawlish .... "	10 9			
	Exeter (St. David's) { arr.	10 25		5 15	
	{ dep.	10 32		6 8	
	Taunton { arr.	11 8		6 12	
	{ dep.	11 14			
170	Weston-super-Mare .. "	11 50			
19	Bristol { Temple Meads { arr.	aft 12 21		7 3	
	{ dep.	12 25		7 20	
	Bristol { Stapleton Rd. 63 "	12 29			
123	Pontypool Road .... "	1 26		8 20	
124	Hereford .... arr.	2 10		9 5	
488	Shrewsbury (General) .... "	3 21		10 20	
489	Crewe .... "	4 10		11 22	
				mrn mrn	
	Crewe .... dep.	4 44		1 12 1 8	
452	Lancaster (Castle) .... arr.	6 10			
454	Carlisle .... "	7 40		4 0 4 5	
455	Lockerbie .... "			4J40 4J44	
	Beattock .... "			4J59 5J4	
730	Carstairs .... "	9 18		5J54 5J56	
731	Motherwell .... "			6J22 6J22	
	Glasgow (Central) .. "	10 0		6 45 6 45	

(C column vertical notes: "Restaurant Car, Weston-super-Mare to Glasgow." — "Teas served between Carlisle and Glasgow." — "Week Day arrivals." — "Sunday arrivals.")

C Through Carriages, Penzance to Glasgow.

D Through Carriages, Plymouth to Glasgow.

F Stops when required.

J Stops to set down on informing the Guard at Carlisle.

A Thro' Carriages, Glasgow to Plymouth.

B Through Carriages, Glasgow to Plymouth daily, and to Penzance except Saturdays.

The Scottish through service called at most of the stations on the route in the Summer of 1930.

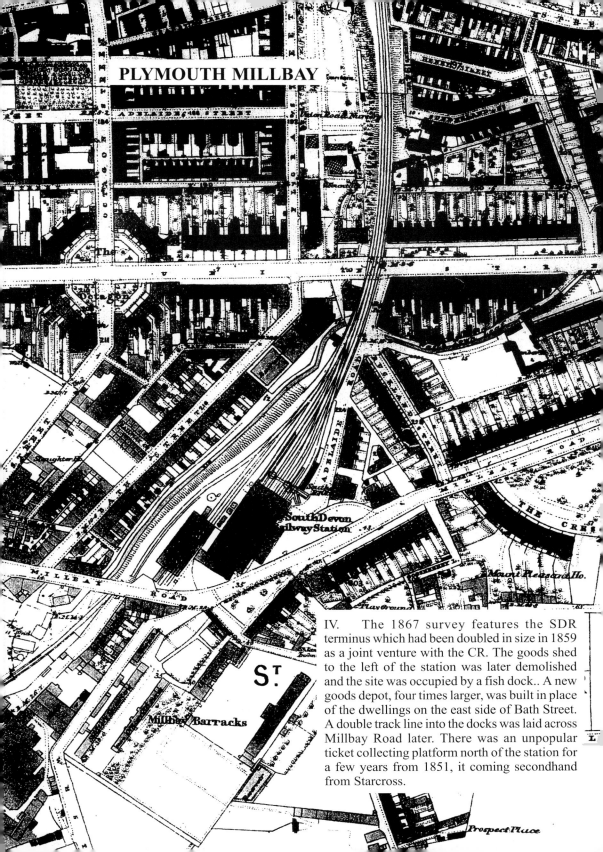

PLYMOUTH MILLBAY

IV. The 1867 survey features the SDR terminus which had been doubled in size in 1859 as a joint venture with the CR. The goods shed to the left of the station was later demolished and the site was occupied by a fish dock.. A new goods depot, four times larger, was built in place of the dwellings on the east side of Bath Street. A double track line into the docks was laid across Millbay Road later. There was an unpopular ticket collecting platform north of the station for a few years from 1851, it coming secondhand from Starcross.

1.   We start our journey in the Great Western Docks and witness an ocean liner express departing from East Quay, the covered station being in the distance. Such through trains to London once operated several times a day, but became rare in the 1960s and the entire route to North Road station closed on 30th June 1971. (R.C.Riley coll.)

2.   This photograph is from 1892; the broad gauge train (centre) may be the last to depart. Note that the outer rail on the left has been severed. The locomotive on the right is standing on the points of the line from the docks, which rises up between the two goods sheds. (LGRP/NRM)

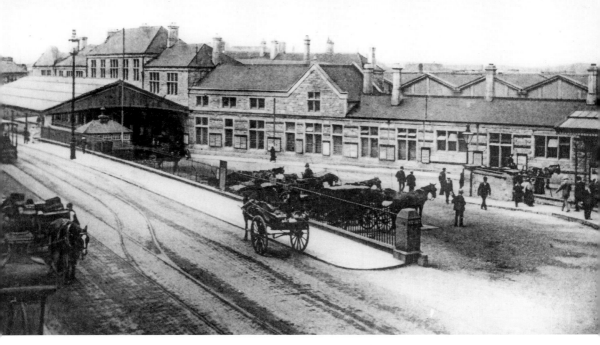

3.   The west elevation is seen after a major rebuild in 1900, when the roof over the platforms, seen in the previous photograph, was removed. The street tramway was in use from 1880 until 1936. An amazing 1,486,581 tickets were issued here in 1913, 0.4m being more common in the 1930s. (Lens of Sutton)

4.   Platforms were sheltered by canopies at their outer ends and by a vaulted roof on lattice girders between the buildings. Evidence of this can be seen in pictures 3 and 6. A local train comprised of two pairs of autocoaches is seen in about 1939 at platform 2. No. 1 was half the length of the others. There had once been a footbridge near the locomotive. (Stations UK)

5.   The platforms were still in place when this southward view was recorded on 28th March 1958. Passenger services were withdrawn abruptly on 23rd April 1941 as a result of severe bombing of the area. The inferno resulted in the incineration of 32 railway cartage horses in their stables. This view is from the 1914 signal box, which had 114 levers and closed on 14th December 1969. The gas tank in the "Short Trilby Siding" provided gas for the restaurant cars. (British Railways)

6.   This picture was taken on 11th September 1958, soon after the removal of the platforms and during their replacement by carriage sidings. On the left is the Duke of Cornwall Hotel, once frequented by passengers changing between trains and transatlantic liners. Carriage berthing was transferred to Laira from 6th October 1969. (British Railways)

Viaduct

Cornwall Railway

SOUTH DEVON

Electric Telegr

Claremont Plac

Boundary
Mark of Ord.

d

Mud

ater Mark of Ordinary Spring Tides

ARUNDEL CRESCENT

Arthur Place

B.M. 74·9

Quarry

56

Durham Cott.

RANK FORT

Melbourne Inn (P.H.)

Engine House Inn (P.H.)

Grosvenor Place

Foundry

V.   This map continues from the previous one and includes the engine shed, which was later extended northwards. The 112yd long Stonehouse Pool Viaduct at the top spans a tidal inlet, which eventually became parkland. Part of Grosvenor Place was demolished to allow depot expansion and housing development soon followed elsewhere.

This station is also featured in
***Branch Line to Launceston
and Princetown
and Branch Lines around
Plymouth.***

Barley House

Belmont Cottages

St. Peter's
Nat School
(Boys)

Statue

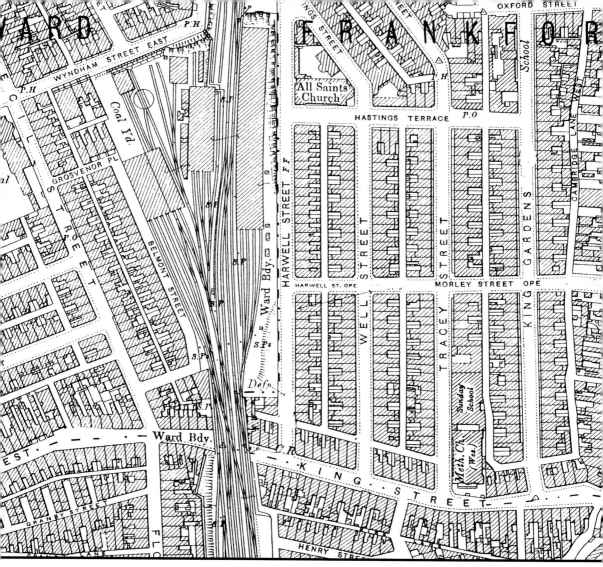

VI. The 1905 survey has the original engine shed in the centre, a later one close to Belmont Street and a carriage shed parallel to Harwell Street. There are four running lines at the bottom edge, the two on the right being for passengers and the next two for goods. The latter were used for passenger trains to the docks after World War II. The engine sheds were closed in 1931 and destroyed in 1941.

Weekday departures December 1938

excluding local trains to Launceston, Plympton, Saltash and Yealmpton

am		pm	
6.10	Liskeard	12.10	Paddington (attached to
7.10	Truro		Cornish Riviera at North Road.)
7.23	St. Germans	12.30	Newton Abbot
7.25	Exeter stopping	1.00	North of England
8.35	Paddington express	1.15	Penzance
8.45	North of England	2.15	Exeter stopping
9.28	Exeter stopping	4.25	Taunton
11.25	Paddington (all	5.15	Exeter stopping
	stations to Exeter)	5.50	Liskeard
11.57	Menheniot	6.15	Bristol
		7.05	Exeter stopping
		7.25	St.Germans
		9.20	Newton Abbot

7.   A northward view of the map area on 28th March 1958 reveals that the yard was used for carriage storage. On the right is the quadruple track from Millbay; Cornwall Junction is in the distance. Harwell Street Signal Box had stood in the left foreground until 4th March 1934, although functioning as a manned ground frame since 1916. (British Railways)

8.   An empty DMU is on the down docks line on 28th August 1961, while an up goods train approaches Cornwall Junction. Left of centre is Belmont Diesel Depot, which was completed in 1958 and closed on 4th October 1964. On the right is the Harwell Street carriage shed. The double track to the docks lasted until 30th June 1971, the others having been taken out of use on 14th December 1969. (R.C.Riley)

9.   Cornwall Junction is seen from a special train running on the final few yards of the former Cornwall Railway route. Looking south on 11th April 1959, we see the two short carriage sidings visible in the right background of picture 7. These, together with the west side of the triangular junction, were dispensed with on 16th January 1964. The signal box had 39 levers and closed on 26th November 1960. (A.E.Bennett)

10.   This northward view of the same location was taken from the special train on the same day as it took ex-SDR curve to North Road. Evident through the wide flat arch carrying North Road itself is the 131yd long Cornwall Loop Viaduct of the main line. Prior to 1896, the signal box was on the site of the hut. (A.E.Bennett)

11.   The line from Millbay is on the left, as is the triangular junction. Clearly seen is the viaduct marked at the top of map V. This panorama is from the top floor of the Divisional Managers Office on 28th September 1963 and it includes the 8.0am Penzance to Plymouth entering North Road and the 11.10 to Portsmouth and Brighton departing. (S.P.Derek)

PLYMOUTH NORTH ROAD

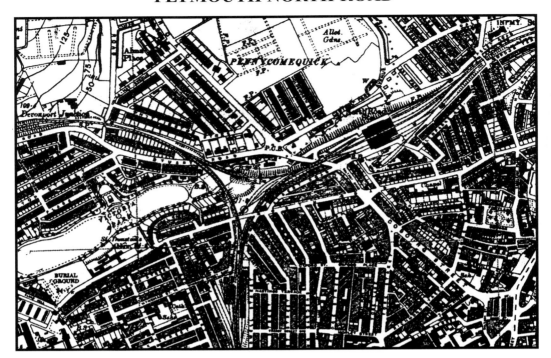

VII.   The 1938 map at 6ins to 1 mile has North Road station right of centre and our route from Millbay at the lower border. On the left is Devonport Junction where the SR and GWR lines diverge. This came into use on 17th May 1876, along with the top part of the triangular junction. The turntable and sidings shown therein were in use from 1913 to 1963. The area of Pennycomequick (top) had a siding laid in 1865 and again in 1873 for agricultural shows.

(lower left)
12.   The LSWR had no station close to the centre of Plymouth and asked the GWR to provide a joint one. After much procrastination, a cheap wooden structure was opened on 28th March 1877. It had two platform lines plus two through lines and was replaced by the station illustrated in 1908. Seen in 1913 from the east, it had four through lines with six platform faces. The locomotive is a "Duke of Cornwall" class 4-4-0. (LGRP/NRM)

13.   The down side shed had two parallel flights of steps on the island platform (left). The combination of gas lights and accumulated smoke made the interior gloomy at night. The first station had a footbridge across four parallel tracks. (British Railways)

14.   No. 4941 *Llangedwyn Hall* arrives from the west in about 1929, the year in which the last reversals at Millbay took place. The parcels office is on the left and West Box is on the right. This was in use from 1908 to 26th November 1960, but had been slid northwards in January 1938, to permit bridge widening. (J.M.Bentley coll.)

15.   All heads were turned on 4th March 1952 as the experimental Metrovick gas turbine no. 18100 arrived on its first trial trip. No. 1006 *County of Cornwall* stands at the end of the platform during signal alterations, the result of which is shown in picture 17. (M.Dart)

16.   The west end of platforms 2 and 3 are shown in 1953, after years of neglect following wartime damage. The footbridge had gone, in favour of a subway (right). Work had started on rebuilding the station in 1938, but was suspended due to World War II. It did not restart until 1956. (British Railways)

17.   Having crossed the viaduct in the right background, no. 4931 *Hanbury Hall* arrives with the up "Royal Duchy" on 13th April 1957. The train was due to depart at 2.0pm, having left Penzance at 11.0am. Paddington arrival time was 7.15pm. (R.K.Blencowe)

18.   Passing over the widened bridge on 30th August 1958 is no. 4936 *Kinlet Hall* with 2-6-0 no. 6319 on the 8.15am Perranporth to Paddington. The line on the left came into use on 23rd April 1954 and was used for empty carriages for Millbay. West Box had 59 levers. (P.W.Gray)

19.   A down ballast train runs through platform 3 on 8th April 1960, as work nears completion on the right. No. 6826 *Nannerth Grange* is near Wymans bookstall, a name once familiar all over the GWR. The suffix "North Road" was dropped on 14th September 1958. (R.C.Riley)

20.   A feature of the west end of the station in this July 1961 photograph is the new panel box (right), which opened on 26th November 1960. On the left is the office block from which picture 11 was taken and which was soon to prove to be greatly in excess of railway requirements. (M.Dart)

This station is also featured in:
Branch Line to Launceston and Princetown (5 to 7), Newton Abbot to Plymouth (110-120) and Tavistock to Plymouth (99-106).

21.   "The Cornishman" has been divided and no. D1026 *Western Centurion* is about to depart with the front portion from platform 2 on 13th October 1972. (There was no platform 1). The centre parts of the tracks at platforms 2 and 3 were removed in 1974 to create four bays and direct pedestrian access to no. 4. (T.Heavyside)

22.   Seen from no. 4 is no. 50035 *Ark Royal*. With the introduction of colour light signalling in 1960, all the lines became reversible. Of the four bays, only the one to the right of the camera was used by passenger trains, usually those to Gunnislake. On the extreme left is platform 8, which was still used by a single sleeping car to and from London in 2001. (Lens of Sutton)

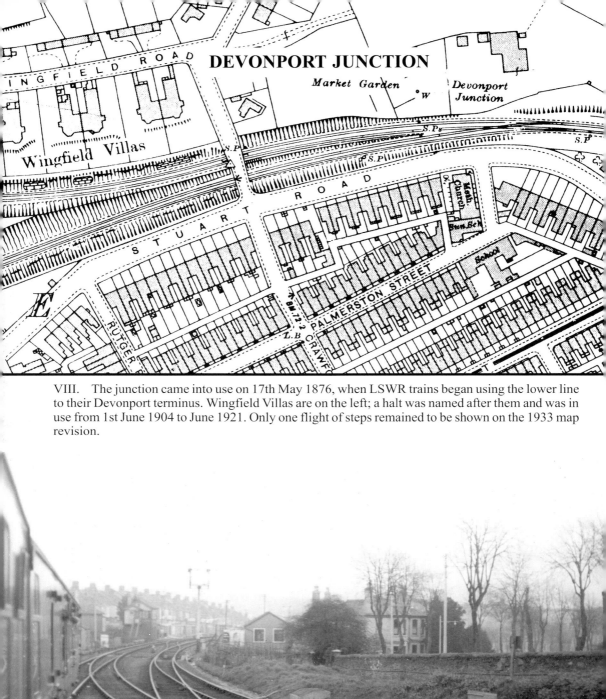

DEVONPORT JUNCTION

Market Garden

Devonport
Junction

Wingfield Villas

STUART ROAD

PALMERSTON STREET

VIII.   The junction came into use on 17th May 1876, when LSWR trains began using the lower line to their Devonport terminus. Wingfield Villas are on the left; a halt was named after them and was in use from 1st June 1904 to June 1921. Only one flight of steps remained to be shown on the 1933 map revision.

←————————

23.   Looking east in bad weather in April 1959, we see the signal box which was in use from 1901 to 26th November 1960. Under the coach had been the points for the siding to Pennycomequick. This was not a medical condition; some believe it to be a corruption of Pen-y-cum-cuick (the valley at the head of the creek), but others refer to a profitable piece of land. (A.E.Bennett)

24.   Colour light signals are in evidence as N class no. 31842 heads the 7.18pm Plymouth to Exeter Central on 14th May 1964. The former LSWR route from here to St. Budeaux was closed to passengers on 7th September 1964, but goods continued to Devonport Kings Road until 4th January 1971. (S.P.Derek)

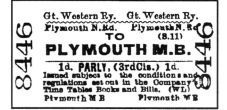

Gt. Western Ry.   Gt. Western Ry.
Plymouth N.Rd.   Plymouth N.Rd
                              (8.11)
PLYMOUTH M.B.
1d. PARLY. (3rdCls.) 1d.
Issued subject to the conditions and
regulations set out in the Company's
Time Tables Books and Bills. (WL)
Plymouth M B   Plymouth W B

8446

Gt. Western Ry   Gt. Western Ry
MUTLEY   MUTLEY
              TO   S.9
DEVONPORT
           (S.R.)
THIRD CLASS
2½d   Fare   2½d
Devonport   Devonport
WK   SEE BACK

4 3 C

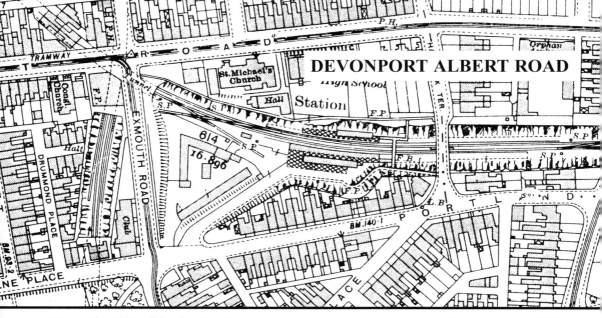

DEVONPORT ALBERT ROAD

IX. The 1933 edition has the SR route lower right and also vertically on the left, near the GWR's tunnel which was 125yds long and received double track in 1899. The original small goods yard is nearby; the one on the right opened on 7th April 1902. The SR's Albert Road Halt was in use from 1st November 1906 to 13th January 1947 and is shown to the left of the GWR station. Devonport was once bigger than the adjacent towns of Plymouth and Stonehouse.

25. The western approach to the station was recorded in 1922, the view including a stairway rising from the footbridge. The map reveals its purpose. The signals on the left control access to the main goods yard. The number of tickets issued in 1903 was 109,507. The figure recorded in 1913 was 302,186 but this included the totals from Dockyard Halt and Ford Halt. (LGRP/NRM)

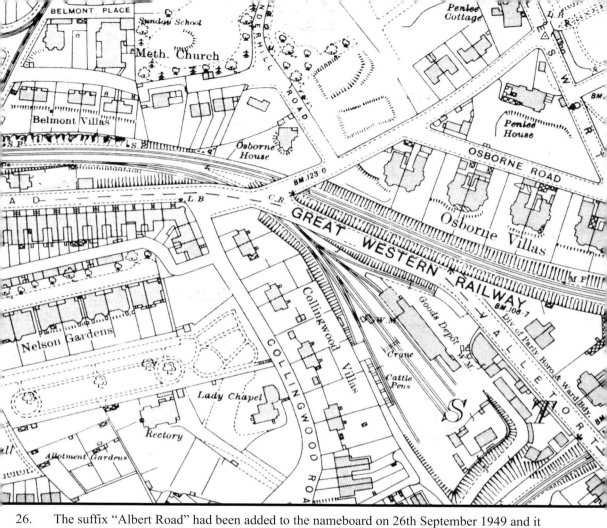

26.   The suffix "Albert Road" had been added to the nameboard on 26th September 1949 and it remained there until 6th May 1968. The station became unstaffed on 19th May 1959. This is an eastward view. (M.Dart coll.)

27.   The 1902 Valletort Road Yard was invisible from passenger trains and is seen in February 1957, along with its 15-ton capacity crane. The yard was closed on 15th April 1957 and traffic transferred to the nearby Southern Region Kings Road depot. (British Railways)

29.   The exterior is pictured on 2nd May 1959, with the entrance to the little used original goods yard on the left. It was officially open for another five years. All buildings were subsequently demolished in favour of two "bus shelters". (R.M.Casserley)

28.   When photographed on 11th September 1958, the yard was being converted to serve as a signal engineers depot. The rail connection was retained until September 1970, after which time road vehicles were used exclusively. (British Railways)

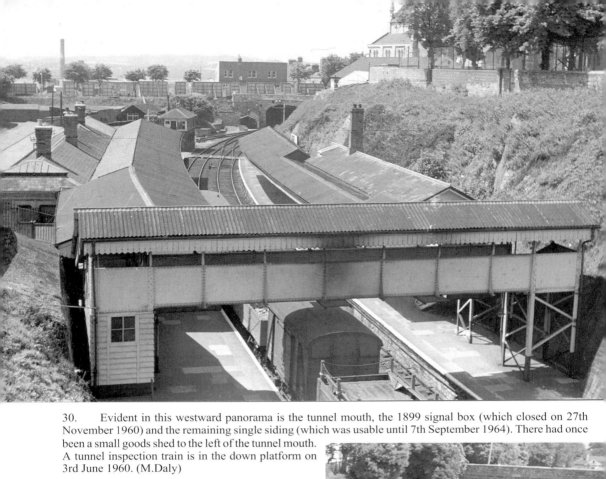

30.   Evident in this westward panorama is the tunnel mouth, the 1899 signal box (which closed on 27th November 1960) and the remaining single siding (which was usable until 7th September 1964). There had once been a small goods shed to the left of the tunnel mouth. A tunnel inspection train is in the down platform on 3rd June 1960. (M.Daly)

31.   The locomotive of this train was no. 4549 and it is seen running round, using the crossovers which were to remain in place until 1964. The line to Valletort Road Yard is on the right. (M.Daly)

DOCKYARD

32. Opened as Dockyard Halt for the railmotor service on 1st June 1905, it still looked new when photographed in 1922. Looking north, Keyham Viaduct and Ford Platform are in the distance. "Halt" was dropped in May 1969; trains still call on weekdays. (LGRP/NRM)

X. The halt is in the centre of this 1933 map and the SR line is on the right.

33.   The 148yd long Keyham Viaduct was photographed in August 1961 from a Southern Region train on Ford Viaduct. The former GWR Ford Halt is on the right. (M.Dart)

FORD HALT

34.   Named "Ford Platform" until 10th July 1922, staff were provided until 1937. This steam railmotor is about to depart north. Workmen were conveyed from 1st June 1904 but other passengers could not travel until 23rd May 1906. (M.Dart coll.)

35.   Propelling its autocoaches to Saltash on 23rd May 1935 is no. 6406. Passengers from the halts could buy their tickets on the train. Closure took place on 6th October 1941, following heavy bombing of the area. (H.C.Casserley)

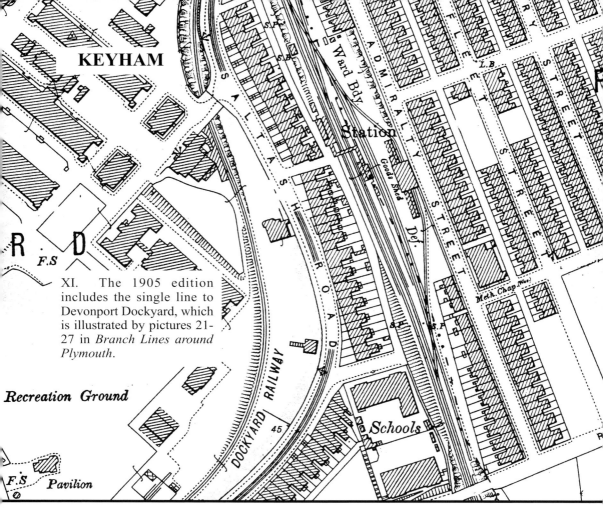

KEYHAM

XI. The 1905 edition includes the single line to Devonport Dockyard, which is illustrated by pictures 21-27 in *Branch Lines around Plymouth*.

Recreation Ground

F.S Pavilion

36. The station opened on 1st January 1900 when the track from the south was doubled. The short sidings shown were provided in 1903. There was a staff of 10 that year, but 14 were employed throughout the 1930s. The up platform is on the right and has an iron hut serving as a waiting "room". (M.Dart coll.)

37.   The sidings had been extended on the east side by the time that this photograph was taken in 1922. The shed on the down side was for parcels. The footbridge was unusual for supporting a loading gauge and for being partially roofed. The up loop could be used by passenger trains. (LGRP/NRM)

38.   No. 4911 *Bowden Hall* suffered a direct hit on 30th April 1941, but the crew survived as they sheltered under the signal box steps. Over 1000 Plymouth residents died while the railway system and docks were devastated in 1940-41. Note the displaced driving wheel. (GWR)

39. The 13.10 Liskeard to Plymouth runs south on 24th February 1972 and passes the signal box, which was in use from 25th June 1900 until 2nd July 1973. The goods yard had closed to general traffic on 19th July 1965, but was retained and used in connection with dockyard movements. (D.H.Mitchell)

40. The dock on the left of the previous picture is on the right of this one and the branch to the Admiralty Dockyard is on the left, beyond the bridge. On trial on the Gunnislake service on 7th July 1981 is prototype railbus no. 140001. (M.Turvey)

(top right)
41. A regular performer on the Gunnislake services was no. 150261 and it is seen departing for Plymouth on 12th November 1998, while no. 59103 waits while stone from Whatley Quarry is unloaded - a rare occurrence. The goods shed followed the other buildings into oblivion in the Summer of 2000, but the loops were retained to facilitate marshalling of stock from the dockyard, where refurbishment contracts are undertaken periodically - see *Branch Lines around Plymouth* pictures 21 to 27. (D.H.Mitchell)

NORTH OF KEYHAM

42.   The agreement for the Admiralty Dockyard connection (left) has been traced back to 15th December 1865. There were links to both up and down lines from 1941 to 1956; the loop line on the left was disconnected in June 1973. No. 7029 *Clun Castle* has just passed over Weston Mill Viaduct on 6th September 1985 with a railtour from Truro. (D.H.Mitchell)

43.   Keyham station is in the right background as no. 50017 *Royal Oak* works a Plymouth - Penzance stopping train on 18th March 1980. Weston Mill Viaduct is 385yds in length and dates from 1903, when this section of the route was doubled. The original alignment was to the east and a footpath on the trackbed led to a walkway across the bridge. (T.Heavyside)

44.   No. 6421 is about 500yds north of Weston Mill Viaduct and is about to pass Ferry Road Junction Box on its way to Saltash. In the foreground is the Admiralty's Bull Point Branch, which was in place from 1916 to 1990 and was used to convey armaments. (M.Daly)

45.   Bull Point Naval Depot had high security and photography was prohibited, however this snap of the internal railway was taken in July 1947. Other such establishments had 18-inch gauge lines; no plans are available. (P.Burkhalter coll.)

46. On the left is the back of Ferry Road signal box (St. Budeaux East until 27th June 1952) and in the foreground is the former SR route. No. 6438 is running towards Saltash, with milk tankers at the rear, in about 1961. (M.Daly)

47. Two photographs taken from the down side of the Western Region main line on 4th August 1964, feature the wartime emergency connection opened between the SR and the GWR on 2nd March 1941. Class N 2-6-0 no. 31845 is hauling empty stock from Millbay to Barnstaple Junction. The signal box closed on 2nd July 1973, having served since 1916. (S.P.Derek)

The other route between Plymouth and St. Budeaux is illustrated in our *Tavistock to Plymouth* album.

48. No. 34079 *141 Squadron* heads the 11.30 from Brighton, which includes a buffet car. Note the connecting lines were not parallel, but that they are being upgraded for regular passenger train use from 7th September 1964, after which date the ex-SR route into Plymouth would be closed. (S.P.Derek)

49. The double track of the connection and of the route to Bere Alston was singled on 7th September 1970. The 13.25 Plymouth to Gunnislake has just joined the single line, having used the crossover from down to up main line on 29th August 1980. Its next stop will be St. Budeaux Victoria Road. (D.H.Mitchell)

ST. BUDEAUX FERRY ROAD

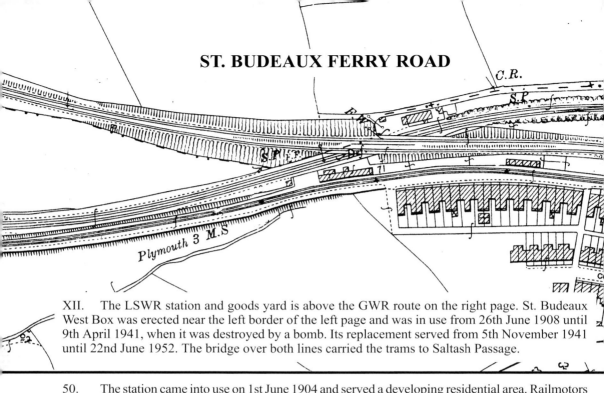

XII.   The LSWR station and goods yard is above the GWR route on the right page. St. Budeaux West Box was erected near the left border of the left page and was in use from 26th June 1908 until 9th April 1941, when it was destroyed by a bomb. Its replacement served from 5th November 1941 until 22nd June 1952. The bridge over both lines carried the trams to Saltash Passage.

50.   The station came into use on 1st June 1904 and served a developing residential area. Railmotors on the new service to Saltash called here. The LSWR tracks are on the left of this 1922 southward view of St. Budeaux Platform. The GWR used this term for a staffed halt. (LGRP/NRM)

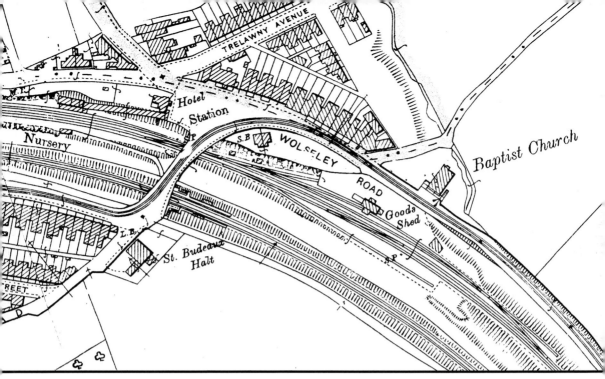

51.   A 1950 look at the up platform shows that the accommodation had been increased. Annual ticket sales had increased from 88,000 in 1923 to 236,000 in 1938, a staff of four being provided. The Southern Region goods shed is in the right background. (E.George/M.Dart)

52.　　No. 4591 waits with an up local train in about 1959. The left banner repeater signal is for the down goods loop, which reached almost to Royal Albert Bridge Box. Victoria Road station is beyond the advertisement hoarding. (M.Daly)

53.　　"Ferry Road" was added to the name on 26th September 1949, plus "Halt" from 18th July 1965 to 5th May 1969. Staffing ceased on the former date, after which time weeds grew on the platform. This photo is from the late 1970s. (Lens of Sutton)

WEST OF ST. BUDEAUX

54.   A down goods loop (right) was provided in 1908 and it remained usable until the down line was taken out of use on 2nd July 1973. Subsequently, single track stretched from St. Budeaux to Saltash, instead of only on the Royal Albert Bridge. We are looking towards Plymouth in June 1965, the bowstring bridge carrying the route over the former SR tracks. (P.Garland/M.Dart)

55.   Our route passes over the ex-SR one yet again in less than half a mile, this time between two of the seven granite piers of the approach spans to the Royal Albert Bridge. A "Hall" class 4-6-0 is bound for Cornwall in 1963. The signal box on the left appears again in the picture after next. (J.H.Moss/R.S.Carpenter)

ROYAL ALBERT BRIDGE

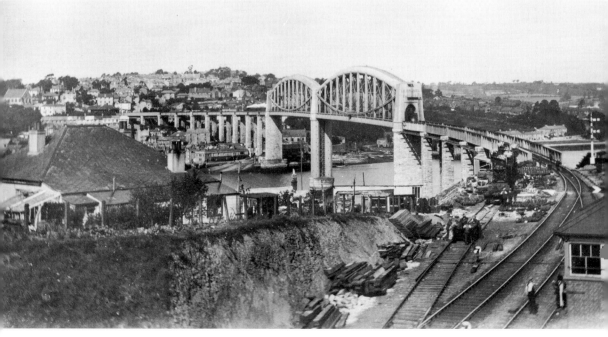

56.   The train ferry was proposed at a location further downstream from the old established vehicular ferry, which was in use until 1961 when the Tamar road bridge opened. The Admiralty had demanded an absurd 100ft headroom, despite few of its large ships venturing inland. Each truss is 455ft in length and contains 1600 tons of wrought iron. (Pamlin Prints)

57.   The foundation of the central pier had to be made on rock over 87ft below high water. To achieve this, an iron cylinder, 35ft diameter, 95ft long and weighing 300 tons, was sunk vertically into the mud. It contained a number of compartments, linked by doorways, which could be pressurised up to 35psi to keep out the water while men laboured inside to establish a firm base and build the masonry. The bends was a condition not understood then and many workers were injured, one fatally. When the tube was sealed at its base, the divisions were removed so that it could act as a coffer dam, instead of a diving bell. The structure is seen in 1928 when a siding was provided opposite Royal Albert Bridge Box for engineers undertaking replacement of the wrought iron approach spans with steel ones. The signal box was operational from 28th June 1908 until 2nd July 1973, since when it has been used by the bridge engineers. (M.Dart coll.)

58.   The two trusses were built on the Devon bank where docks were provided under each end of each one. In each of these there was a pontoon (effectively a floating box, the buoyancy of which could be altered by pumps) carrying a massive timber cradle (foreground). Each truss was topped by an elliptical tube formed from wrought iron plates. The western truss was floated out to the stumps of the piers on 1st September 1857, watched by about 40,000 people, who were ordered to maintain silence during the operation. Commands were given verbally by Brunel through a network of assistants and also by the use of flags. The tide dropped and allowed the truss to be lowered onto the pier bases. Hydraulic jacks were then used to raise it about 6ft per week; on the shore pier, masonry was built up and the central pier was created using 14ft high iron castings. The Cornish truss was raised to its final position in July 1858 and the nearest was in place in March 1859. (Lens of Sutton)

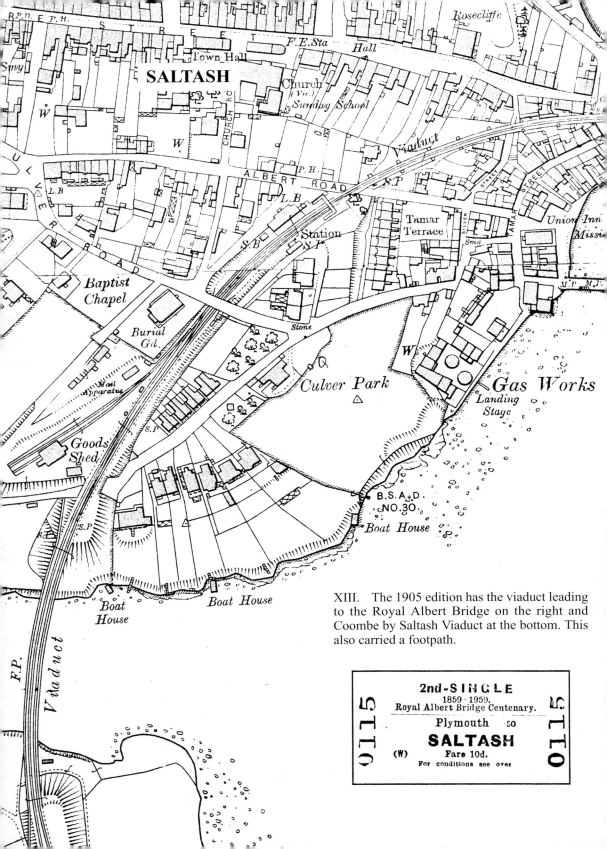

SALTASH

XIII. The 1905 edition has the viaduct leading to the Royal Albert Bridge on the right and Coombe by Saltash Viaduct at the bottom. This also carried a footpath.

2nd-SINGLE
1859 - 1959.
Royal Albert Bridge Centenary.
Plymouth   to
SALTASH
(W)   Fare 10d.
For conditions see over

0115   0115

59.   The station was rebuilt in 1880 and is seen here with broad gauge track. The dock siding on the left was lost during the gauge conversion of 1892. A crossbar signal is evident at the end of the down platform. The points were moved 66yds nearer the bridge in March 1908, by widening the viaduct. (M.Dart coll.)

60.   The success of the 1904 railmotor scheme meant that longer trains were required. This necessitated extension of the up platform, which meant provision of a longer road bridge. We witness demolition of the arch in 1906. There was a substantial flower traffic from this station for many years. (M.Dart coll.)

ROAD MOTORS.
SALTASH, CALLINGTON, and ALBASTON.—Great Western.

Saltash.....dep.	....	9 45	1130	2 30	....	4*40	5 25	....	8815		aft	Albaston.....dep.	7b45	1115	3c10	6 20	7d15	....	....	aft
Callington......	7b15	1045	1240	3c30	2c45	5*45	6 35	6d45	9s15		4 0	Callington.....	8 25	1145	3 45	6 45	7d40	8 s 0		8 0
Albaston...arr.	7b40	1110	....	3 55	3c10	6 10	....	7d10	....		aft	Saltash......arr.	9 25	1245	4 45	7 45	....	9 s 0		9 0

b Mons. & Sats.   *c* Wednesdays & Saturdays.   *d* Wednesdays only.   *s* Sats. only.   * Except Wednesdays & Saturdays.

61. From 1876, the railway was subsidising a road service to Callington, using a four-horse coach. The GWR employed four "motor cars" to run the 14 miles to Albaston from 1st June 1904. The inset timetable is from October 1905. (M.Dart coll.)

62. A 1922 photograph includes the 1906 road bridge and the extension of the building, completed in 1908. The station was gas lit and adorned with palms. Expansion of traffic resulted in staff increasing from 14 in 1903 to 21 in 1923. (LGRP/NRM)

63. New and larger railmotors were introduced in 1905, but they soon proved inadequate resulting in autotrains of this type being provided from 1909. Initially the small 0-6-0Ts were encased to match the coaches, but this lasted only until 1911. Here we see the autotrain at its optimum length and in its final form in July 1959. (Photomatic)

64. The autotrains were replaced by DMUs during the demise of steam in the early 1960s. No. W51329 is seen during layover in the goods yard on 23rd September 1960. No. 4087 *Cardigan Castle* is recovering from a signal check while working the 6.55am Penzance to Paddington. (R.C.Riley)

65.   The goods yard closed on 9th September 1963, but the track remained in place for layovers until 1972. Class 25 no. 7677 leads class 52 no. D1026 *Western Centurion* on 31st May 1973, as new cable trunking is ready for colour light signals. The semaphores and the signal box seen in picture no. 62 ceased to be used after 2nd July 1973. The goods shed was in commercial use in 2000. (G.Gillham)

66.   The Tamar Bridge opened for road traffic on 24th October 1961 and was widened in 2000-01. Two class 158 units enter the down platform on 2nd August 1993 while forming the 12.00 Cardiff to Penzance service. The building had ceased to be staffed on 11th October 1971 and was subsequently fenced off for private use. (P.G.Barnes)

67.   There were originally 22 timber-built viaducts from here to St. Austell and they were gradually replaced, except the two west of Coombe by Saltash Viaduct, which is seen here. Those two were eliminated following the completion of the new route further inland in 1908. The structure carrying the HST was completed in 1894. There was a down goods loop west of it from 1943 to 1972. (M.Turvey)

EAST OF ST. GERMANS

68.   The 17-arch St. Germans Viaduct dates from 1907 and is seen bearing the 07.25 Paddington to Penzance HST on 30th July 1981. It has just passed over the 28-arch Nottar Viaduct, which is 206yds in length. (D.H.Mitchell)

XIV.   Evidence of the earlier route is shown as earthworks on the 1946 edition at 1ins to 1 mile. Some of these, together with stonework, can still be seen today. Also marked is the 451yd long Shillingham Tunnel on the new route. Defiance Halt was situated near the east end of the diversion and was in use, mainly by the Naval Torpedo School, from 1st March 1905 until 23rd October 1930. Records show a staff of four usually and average annual ticket sales of 30,000. Between the east end of the diversion and the west end of the down goods loop was Wearde signal box. It was in use from 1908 until October 1965, when the loop became a siding. A two-arch road bridge still shows the point of divergence of the two routes at their east end.

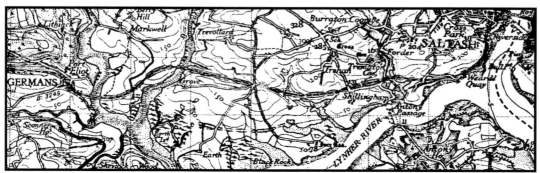

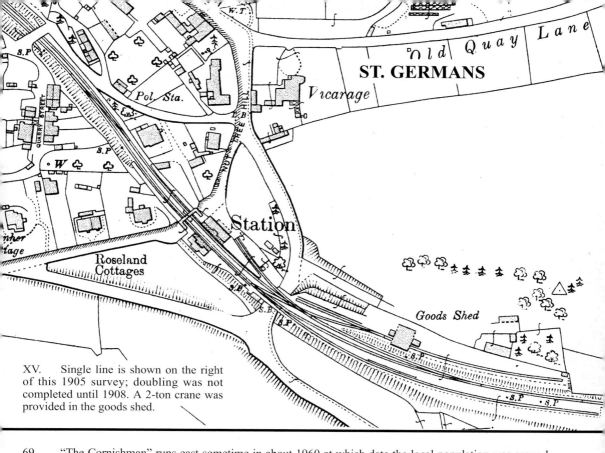

XV.   Single line is shown on the right of this 1905 survey; doubling was not completed until 1908. A 2-ton crane was provided in the goods shed.

69.   "The Cornishman" runs east sometime in about 1960 at which date the local population was around 1800 souls. Construction of a branch to Looe from St. Germans was started in 1938 - see *Branch Line to Looe*. There were 9 or 10 men employed here in the 1930s. (J.H.Moss/R.S.Carpenter)

70. The goods yard closed on 19th July 1965, but the down refuge siding (right of centre) was in use until February 1966. The signal box lasted until 6th May 1973 when the panel controlling the few colour light signals was moved into the room at the east end of the down platform building. (J.H.Moss/R.S.Carpenter)

71. Centre is the room that housed the small panel until 26th April 1998, when its functions were transferred to the signal box at Liskeard and to Plymouth Panel. All the buildings were well conserved in 2000, the up side being used as a dwelling offering bed and breakfast. An LSWR van had been placed in the bay on the right, it serving to increase the accommodation. The photograph dates from June 1966. (C.L.Caddy)

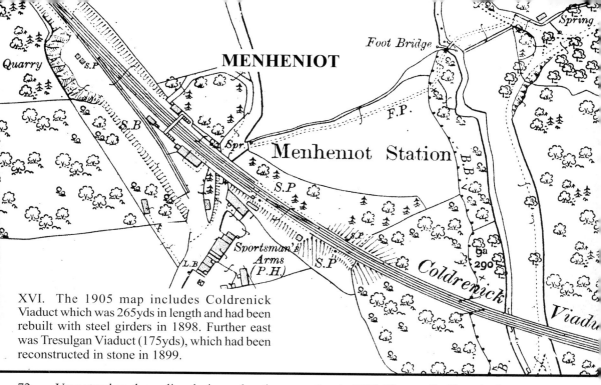

MENHENIOT

XVI. The 1905 map includes Coldrenick Viaduct which was 265yds in length and had been rebuilt with steel girders in 1898. Further east was Tresulgan Viaduct (175yds), which had been reconstructed in stone in 1899.

72.   Vans stand on the up line during a shunting operation in 1922. The small village is about one mile north of the station and so generated minimal passenger traffic. However, a staff of six was required at this time. (LGRP/NRM)

73.   Initially the chalet-style building was accompanied by a loop and a single siding. The quarry hoppers are evident as no. 7916 *Mobberley Hall* speeds through with the 1.20pm Penzance to Paddington on 16th July 1956. Station staffing ceased on 26th April 1965. (R.C.Riley)

74.   The goods yard closed on 9th September 1963, but the siding to the stone quarry was in use until the end of 1969, it having been laid down in 1931 principally for the conveyance of railway ballast. No. 6838 *Goodmoor Grange* is working the "North Mail" on the same day. (R.C.Riley)

75.   No. 47621 has descended the 1 in 80 gradient into the station and is stopping to collect a few passengers on 24th April 1985. The signal box had closed on 30th September 1973, but was still in use as a track staff mess room more than 25 years later. The shelter on the right was still standing in 2000. (G.Gillham)

76.   No. 1023 *County of Oxford* is running over the 240yd long Liskeard Viaduct with the 10.40am Paddington to Penzance on 10th July 1959. The Looe branch is concealed below it. The train has just passed over Bolitho Viaduct (182yds) and Cartuther Viaduct (162yds). (R.C.Riley)

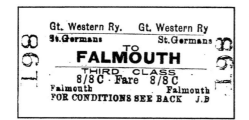

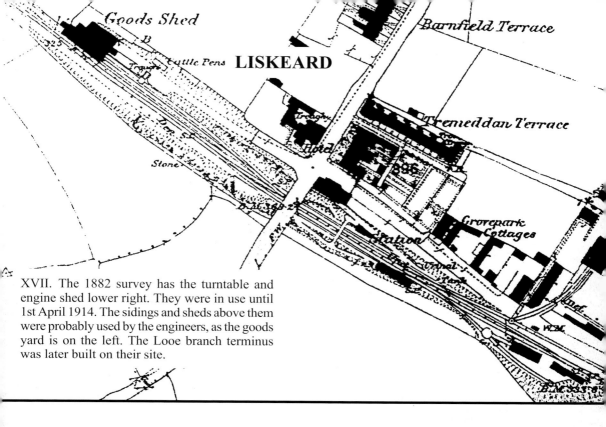

Goods Shed

Barnfield Terrace

Cattle Pens **LISKEARD**

Tremeddan Terrace

Stone

Grovepark Cottages

Station

XVII. The 1882 survey has the turntable and engine shed lower right. They were in use until 1st April 1914. The sidings and sheds above them were probably used by the engineers, as the goods yard is on the left. The Looe branch terminus was later built on their site.

77.   The down platform had the larger building and is seen with 13 of the employees. The payroll showed 17 in 1903, 22 in 1913 and 30 in 1923. (Lens of Sutton)

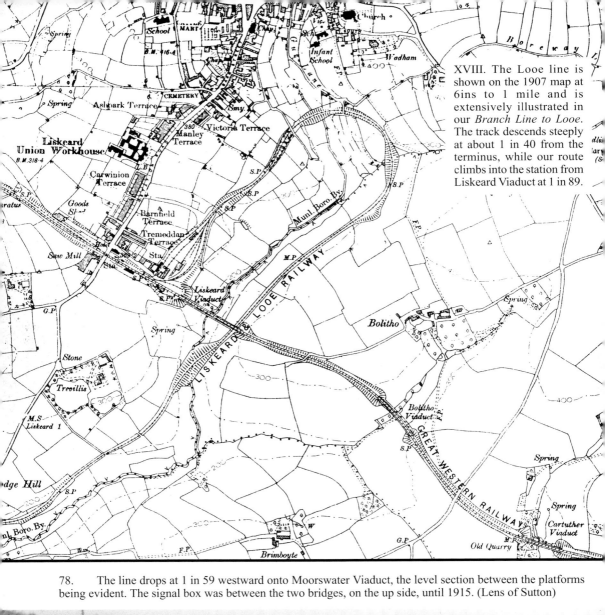

XVIII. The Looe line is shown on the 1907 map at 6ins to 1 mile and is extensively illustrated in our *Branch Line to Looe*. The track descends steeply at about 1 in 40 from the terminus, while our route climbs into the station from Liskeard Viaduct at 1 in 89.

78. The line drops at 1 in 59 westward onto Moorswater Viaduct, the level section between the platforms being evident. The signal box was between the two bridges, on the up side, until 1915. (Lens of Sutton)

79.   No. 6800 *Arlington Grange* is passing through with a down parcels train in the Summer of 1960. The main building and ticket office is top left; the access to the goods yard is also on the left. (R.S.Carpenter)

80.   The hillside supply to the water tank is evident in this panorama from 18th July 1960. No. 4552 will soon put the three wagons in a siding and take the rest of the train to St. Blazey, where the Looe branch coaches will be cleaned. Goods traffic here ceased in June 1981. (R.C.Riley)

81.   On the left is the footpath to the branch platform. No. 37673 is bringing clay hopper wagons off the branch on 28th April 1988, the wagons having been loaded at Moorswater. The connection was to the down line until June 1981, but the arrangement seen gave direct access to the branch for trains of empty wagons from the west. (G.Gillham)

82.   "Sprinter" no. 155325 formed the 11.39 from Penzance on 23rd April 1990. The 1984 extension of the up platform can be seen; in 2000 a footpath was laid alongside it to give access to a new car park on the goods yard site. Mechanical signalling and point operation continued into the 21st century. (G.Gillham)

WEST OF LISKEARD

83.   A class 47 hauls the St. Blazey to Severn Tunnel Junction Speedlink services across Moorswater Viaduct (318yds) on 28th April 1987. Below is the line to Moorswater, where clay was loaded until April 1997. The track remained unused until June 1999, when cement trains began to arrive regularly. The stumps of the original viaduct have stood idle since 1881. Two miles to the east there was an up goods loop at Tremabe from 1943 until 1952. (P.G.Barnes)

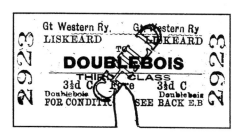

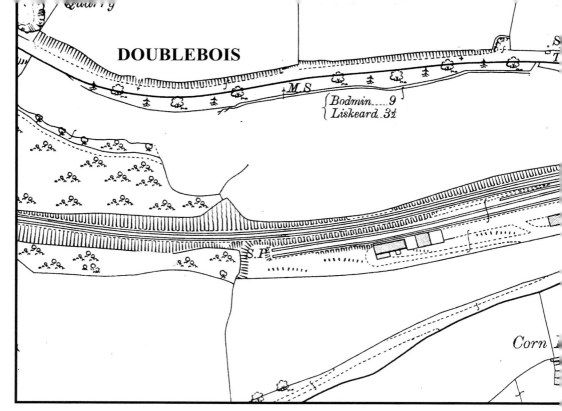

DOUBLEBOIS

M.S

{ Bodmin......9
{ Liskeard..3¼

S.P

Corn

84.   An eastward view in 1922 features the signal box, which was operational from 1894 until 11th January 1968. There were 7 or 8 men engaged here throughout the 1920s and 30s. (LGRP/NRM)

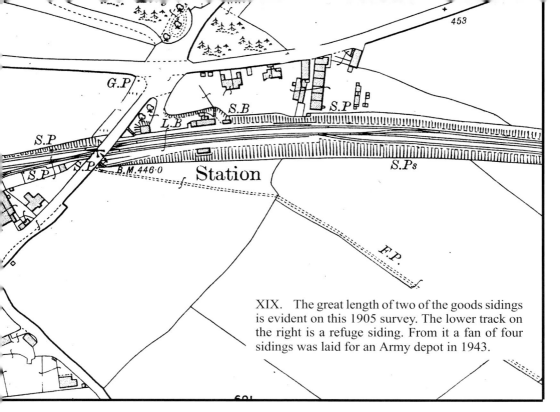

XIX. The great length of two of the goods sidings is evident on this 1905 survey. The lower track on the right is a refuge siding. From it a fan of four sidings was laid for an Army depot in 1943.

85.   Change was slow at a rural outpost such as this. A Cornwall Railway notice was still to be seen on 23rd May 1935. There were very few residents in the vicinity to observe it. Here is more evidence of flower traffic. (H.C.Casserley)

86.   A down goods train has been left on the up line during shunting in 1947. On the right is the headshunt for the ammunition sidings, which are out of view to the right of the locomotive. These lines were later used for track panel assembly, but became redundant in 1968. On the west end of the main building is a letter box, recorded as L.B. on the map. (LGRP/NRM)

87.   The goods yard, cattle pens and 2-ton crane were also recorded in 1947. The main line is dropping away at 1 in 66 towards Westwood Viaduct, which is 85yds in length. An extremely long sand drag is provided in its vicinity on the down line, east of the single line section over St. Pinnock Viaduct (202yds) and Largin Viaduct (177yds). Several recent disasters could have been avoided by use of this simple device. (LGRP/NRM)

88.   No. 5021 *Whittington Castle* passes with the up "Royal Duchy" on 4th July 1959. Passenger traffic here dwindled and service was withdrawn on 5th October 1964. Freight traffic ceased on 7th December following. (P.W.Gray)

WEST OF DOUBLEBOIS

89.   St. Pinnock Viaduct is seen on 6th July 1955 as no. 6873 *Caradoc Grange* works the 11.0am from Penzance and passes no. 5003 *Lulworth Castle* (right) hauling a down excursion from Exeter. Singling of over half a mile of the route took place on 24th May 1964, the measure being taken to reduce the weight on the lattice structures. A signal box at Largin was in use periodically between 1906 and 1991, while another at Onslow Siding served a clay kiln in 1931-68. (R.C.Riley)

BODMIN PARKWAY

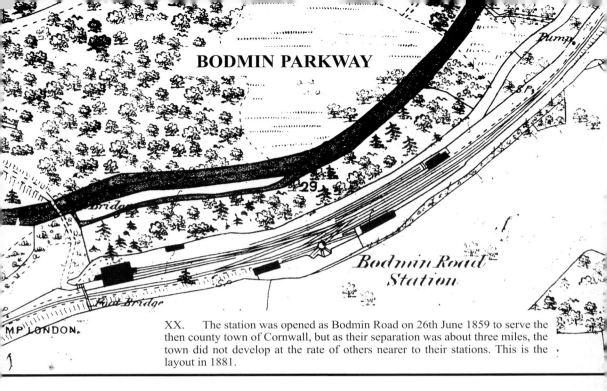

XX.   The station was opened as Bodmin Road on 26th June 1859 to serve the then county town of Cornwall, but as their separation was about three miles, the town did not develop at the rate of others nearer to their stations. This is the layout in 1881.

90.   The new branch platform, covered footbridge and signal box were recorded in about 1890. Between 4th May and 26th June 1859, passengers had to use the private halt at Respryn, west of the station. The signal box was in regular use until 30th November 1983; it eventually became a buffet. (BWR)

91.   A westward panorama in 1922 includes the goods shed and the unusual cantilevered water supply for locomotives. There was usually a staff of 12 here between the wars. (LGRP/NRM)

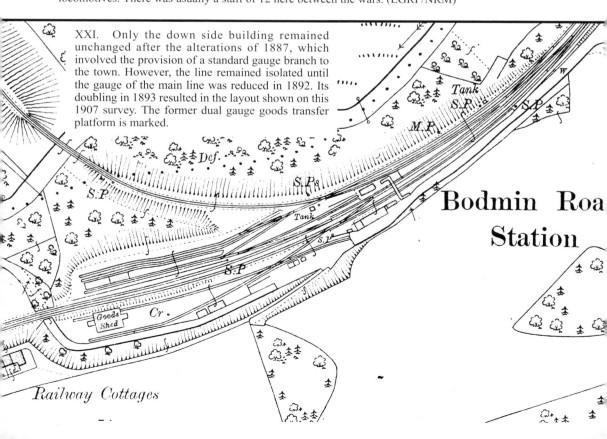

XXI.   Only the down side building remained unchanged after the alterations of 1887, which involved the provision of a standard gauge branch to the town. However, the line remained isolated until the gauge of the main line was reduced in 1892. Its doubling in 1893 resulted in the layout shown on this 1907 survey. The former dual gauge goods transfer platform is marked.

Bodmin Roa
Station

92.   A closer view of the goods shed includes the first part of the branch to Bodmin General, where trains reversed for Padstow. The line through the goods shed continued to a private siding from 1920 until 1966, although general freight traffic ceased on 4th November 1963. The siding had initially served clay dries and latterly a Naval store. (Lens of Sutton)

93.   No. 7925 *Westol Hall* accelerates a down train on 17th August 1959, dropping at 1 in 65 past the level sidings. Those on the left were not lifted, being retained for transfer traffic to and from the branch. (P.Hay)

94.   The Plymouth Railway Circle and the Railway Correspondence & Travel Society combined to run "The Cornubian" to mark the end of steam to Penzance on 3rd May 1964. No. 34002 *Salisbury* of the SR "West Country" class was in charge, although this type was not normally used on the route. (S.C.Nash)

95.   A train of loaded clay wagons stands on the down line, while its locomotive can be seen at the branch platform. Trains carrying clay from Wenford to Fowey had to reverse here and at Bodmin General. The branch was closed to passengers on 30th January 1967 and to all traffic on 3rd October 1983. (Lens of Sutton)

Other views of this station and of the BWR can be found in *Branch Lines around Bodmin* and in *Wenford Bridge to Fowey*.

96.   The name was changed from Bodmin Road to Bodmin Parkway on 4th November 1983. An 11-coach relief train on Easter Monday 27th April 1984 was hauled by no. 50003 *Temeraire*. The points under the two leading coaches were taken out of use on 30th May 1985, when the 36-lever signal box was closed, but a connection to the branch was retained at the other end of the platform. (G.Gillham)

97.　　Although Honiton is indicated, this DMU is departing for Penzance on 24th September 1990 and is passing the two new buildings that were completed in 1989. On the left is a locomotive on the Bodmin & Wenford Railway, which completed the reopening of the branch on 17th June 1990 and regularly runs steam trains. (M.Turvey)

98.　　In the foreground is the one remaining connection, which was still used in 2001 for transfer wagons to and from Fitzgerald Lighting of Bodmin. A train is departing for Bodmin General on 24th September 1990, hauled by 0-4-0ST no. 19, formerly used at Devonport Dockyard (M.Turvey)

LOSTWITHIEL

Corn Mᴸ

Stone

Tank

Station

LOSTWITHIEL

Town Quay

Norway House

Carriage Works

XXII. Unlike Bodmin Road, this station opened with the line and was close to the town centre. The CR established its carriage and wagon works here. The adjacent water frontage would have been useful for off-loading water-borne materials. Note the fan of tramway sidings near the railway bridge over the River Fowey, which is tidal to this town. Horses hauled iron ore from a mine near Restormel Castle to the quay from 1836 to 1883. The right hand line at the bottom of this 1881 map was used for minerals only from 1869 to 1880. It reopened in 1895 and carried passengers as well thereafter. The main line was doubled southwards to Milltown Viaduct (144yds) in 1896. Beyond that, there had been two tracks to Par since 1894, these passing through the 565yd long Treverrin Tunnel. There was a signal box near its east portal from 1911 to 1956.

99.   The station was improved in the 1890s with canopies, a footbridge and a third platform face (left) for Fowey branch trains. A shunter adopts a classic pose with his pole in 1922. (LGRP/NRM)

100.   Looking in the other direction in 1935, we see one of the hills flanking the beautiful wooded Fowey Valley through which we have descended. To have been greeted by palms upon arrival, would have pleased many weary travellers. (H.C.Casserley)

XXIII. The 1907 edition reveals the extra lines laid north of the level crossing. The slaughter house is conveniently close to the cattle dock for all except the quadrupeds. Carriage and wagon repair work continued long after the demise of the CR. The signal box near the goods shed was called Lostwithiel Branch Box and was in use from 1895 to 1923. The Fowey branch is the right one of the three tracks at the lower border, but has branched off south of the bridge since 1972.

101.   No. 4907 *Broughton Hall* arrives with the 2.55pm Plymouth North Road to Truro stopping train on 22nd May 1935. The signal box dates from 1893 and was still in use in 2001, although only 39 of its 63 levers functioned. There were about 14 employees here in the 1930s. (H.C.Casserley)

102.   Vans stand at the cattle dock as no. 5011 *Tintagel Castle* drifts over the crossing in the 1950s. The milk depot in the background was provided with a siding in 1932. The bus is Western National, a company in which the GWR had a large holding. (M.Dart coll.)

103.   The 10.20 Penzance to Newcastle has just passed over the River Fowey on a new bridge on 28th April 1983. The former CR building is on the right and sidings for china clay trains are on the left. Public freight traffic ceased on 1st June 1964. (T.Heavyside)

104.   No. 37185 has passed the station and runs into the up loop with loaded Burngullow-Fowey "clay hoods" on 24th April 1984. Here the locomotive will run-round. It carries the Red Lizard symbol of "Cornish Railways", a separate division of the WR which had been set up in July 1983 and based in Truro. Unfortunately it had a very short lifespan, being abolished two years later. In the background is the large milk processing plant which once provided considerable rail traffic until this was transferred to the roads in the early 1980s. The rake of refurbished milk tank wagons visible here proved to be a waste of money, as many were subsequently scrapped without being used. (G.Gillham)

PAR

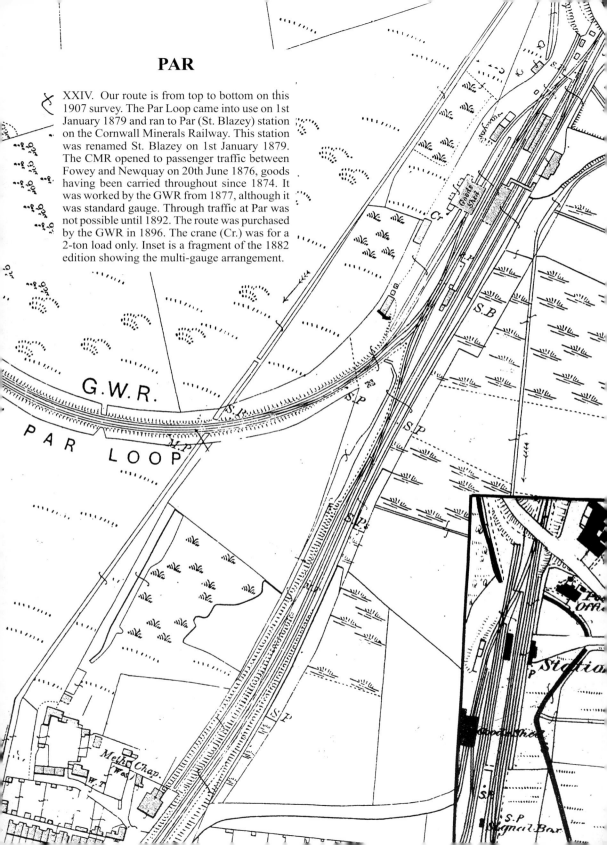

XXIV. Our route is from top to bottom on this 1907 survey. The Par Loop came into use on 1st January 1879 and ran to Par (St. Blazey) station on the Cornwall Minerals Railway. This station was renamed St. Blazey on 1st January 1879. The CMR opened to passenger traffic between Fowey and Newquay on 20th June 1876, goods having been carried throughout since 1874. It was worked by the GWR from 1877, although it was standard gauge. Through traffic at Par was not possible until 1892. The route was purchased by the GWR in 1896. The crane (Cr.) was for a 2-ton load only. Inset is a fragment of the 1882 edition showing the multi-gauge arrangement.

G.W.R.

PAR LOOP

Meth. Chap.

105.   An up train is arriving while a train from St. Blazey waits on the right during the 1903 floods. The adjacent building was built as the "tranship shed" and had tracks of different gauges until 1892. (M.Dart coll.)

106.   A 1922 panorama includes platform extensions, the island one having been lengthened in 1913. There was a buffet on this one. The goods yard remained in use until 1st October 1964. The middle door post of the shed was still off centre, reflecting its dual gauge origin. There was a staff of around 24 between the wars. (LGRP/NRM)

107.   The main line west is on the left as a Large Prairie 2-6-2T arrives with a train from Newquay in May 1959. It has just used the crossover at the end of the double track from St. Blazey. (R.S.Carpenter)

108.   The east elevation was recorded in July 1963, remarkably uncluttered by motor cars. The ticket office was still in use at the end of the 20th century. (Lens of Sutton)

109.   Devoid of a headboard, "Warship" class no. D807 *Caradoc* arrives with the down "Cornish Riviera Express" at 3.32pm on 28th May 1961. Paddington departure was at 10.30am. The connections under the bridge were altered in 1962 to the arrangement shown in picture 112. (T.Heavyside)

110.   The structure dates from 1890, although it is on the site of the smaller 1879 box. The 57-lever frame from 1913 was still in use in 2001, although a panel had been added in 1965 to extend control west to Probus. The platform had been lengthened in front of the box in 1913. (C.L.Caddy)

111.   No. 50012 *Benbow* and Mk.I coaches were being used in place of a failed HST for a London service on 14th June 1984. A DMU waits to leave for Newquay, while no. 45037 is ready to depart with the 15.15 St. Blazey to Severn Tunnel Junction freight. Signal engineers occupied the goods yard site by that time. (G.Gillham)

112.   A class 37 is approaching the bidirectionally signalled platform loop line with empty clay wagons from Fowey on 30th April 1984. On the right is the down loop, which had been only a siding until 1943. (P.G.Barnes)

113.   More "clay hoods" are seen, this time approaching from the west behind no. 50003 *Temeraire* on 1st May 1987. They are descending at 1 in 57, having just run past the steaming clay dries and above the single line to Par Harbour. Known as "Chapel Siding", the line on the right was used for berthing DMUs and for fuelling locomotives of clay trains awaiting a path to Lostwithiel. (P.G.Barnes)

ST. AUSTELL GOODS

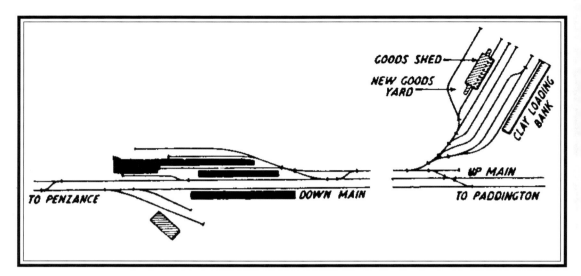

XXV. St.Austell's third goods depot was ¼ mile east of the station and opened on 2nd November 1931. It had a 5-ton crane. Most of the earlier sidings were retained.

114.   No. 5985 *Mostyn Hall* is working hard on the 1 in 60 gradient on 7th July 1956 and almost obscures the connection to the reversible line, which continued to the station. The yard ceased to take general goods on 6th May 1968, but some complete loads were handled until about 1985. (M.Dart)

115.   No. 47293 accelerates rapidly with the 16.42 St. Erth to Clapham Junction milk train on 26th July 1979. The loop had ceased to exist, but the track was still available in 2001 for berthing an HST in an emergency. (D.H.Mitchell)

116.   The yard run-round loop was used by Motorail trains. No. 47297 is propelling on 9th June 1984, prior to pushing its train back to the station for unloading. Motorail services from here were last operated to London in 1984, to Crewe in 1980, to Worcester in 1978 and to Dover in 1975. (G.Gillham)

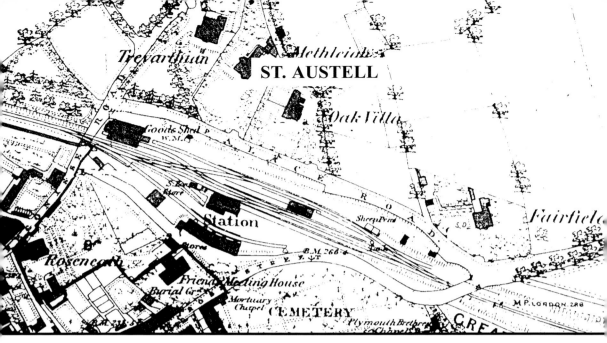

XXV1. The first goods shed was north of the main line, as indicated on this 1881 map of the broad gauge layout. A footbridge was added in 1882.

117.   A 1922 westward panorama reveals the location of the second and much larger goods shed. The cattle pens can also be seen. The staff of 27 in 1923 increased to 40 for most of the 1930s. (LGRP/NRM)

118.   The close association of the railway with Western National is evident in this view from 1st June 1960. No. 1008 *County of Cardigan* is departing with the 1.30pm Paddington to Penzance. The nearest siding on the left was removed in 1971 to permit platform lengthening, the one on the extreme right went in 1965 to benefit the bus operator and the other one vanished in 1979. (M.Dart)

119.   On the left under the bridge is the commencement of the reversible line to the 1931 goods depot. About to depart east on 11th May 1968 is no. D1067 *Western Druid*. A five-lever ground frame controlled the crossovers in 2001. (C.L.Caddy)

120.   No. 25207 passes with a Truro to Plymouth Friary freight on 16th August 1978. There had been a level crossing just beyond the signal box until 21st September 1931. It was replaced by the footbridge, which came from the then recently closed station at St. Blazey. The 43-lever box was the third here and closed on 22nd March 1980. The building on the right was for the use of Motorail passengers. (D.H.Mitchell)

121.   A long train of mail and newspaper vans stands at the up platform on 23rd June 1987, while "Skipper" unit no. 142023 is about to bounce down to Penzance. The main building was demolished on 30th November 1999 and a spacious new booking hall was opened on 8th June 2000. Hopefully, passenger figures will continue to rise as rail revival seems set to continue. (G.Gillham)

MP Middleton Press

Easebourne Lane, Midhurst, W Sussex. GU29 9AZ Tel: 01730 813169 Fax: 01730 812601
*If books are not available from your local transport stockist, order direct with cheque,
Visa or Mastercard, post free UK.*

BRANCH LINES
Branch Line to Allhallows
Branch Line to Alton
Branch Lines around Ascot
Branch Line to Ashburton
Branch Lines around Bodmin
Branch Line to Bude
Branch Lines around Canterbury
Branch Lines around Chard & Yeovil
Branch Line to Cheddar
Branch Lines around Cromer
Branch Lines to East Grinstead
Branch Lines of East London
Branch Lines to Effingham Junction
Branch Lines around Exmouth
Branch Line to Fairford
Branch Lines around Gosport
Branch Line to Hawkhurst
Branch Lines to Horsham
Branch Lines around Huntingdon
Branch Line to Ilfracombe
Branch Line to Kingswear
Branch Lines to Launceston & Princetown
Branch Lines to Longmoor
Branch Line to Looe
Branch Line to Lyme Regis
Branch Lines around March
Branch Lines around Midhurst
Branch Line to Minehead
Branch Line to Moretonhampstead
Branch Lines around North Woolwich
Branch Line to Padstow
Branch Lines around Plymouth
Branch Lines to Seaton and Sidmouth
Branch Line to Selsey
Branch Lines around Sheerness
Branch Line to Shrewsbury
Branch Line to Swanage *updated*
Branch Line to Tenterden
Branch Lines around Tiverton
Branch Lines to Torrington
Branch Lines to Tunbridge Wells
Branch Line to Upwell
Branch Lines of West London
Branch Lines around Weymouth
Branch Lines around Wisbech

NARROW GAUGE
Branch Line to Lynton
Branch Lines around Portmadoc 1923-46
Branch Lines around Porthmadog 1954-94
Branch Line to Southwold
Douglas to Port Erin
Kent Narrow Gauge
Two-Foot Gauge Survivors
Romneyrail
Southern France Narrow Gauge
Vivarais Narrow Gauge

SOUTH COAST RAILWAYS
Ashford to Dover
Bournemouth to Weymouth
Brighton to Eastbourne
Brighton to Worthing
Dover to Ramsgate
Eastbourne to Hastings
Hastings to Ashford
Portsmouth to Southampton
Southampton to Bournemouth

SOUTHERN MAIN LINES
Basingstoke to Salisbury
Bromley South to Rochester
Crawley to Littlehampton
Dartford to Sittingbourne
East Croydon to Three Bridges
Epsom to Horsham
Exeter to Barnstaple
Exeter to Tavistock
Faversham to Dover

London Bridge to East Croydon
Orpington to Tonbridge
Tonbridge to Hastings
Salisbury to Yeovil
Swanley to Ashford
Tavistock to Plymouth
Victoria to Bromley South
Victoria to East Croydon
Waterloo to Windsor
Waterloo to Woking
Woking to Portsmouth
Woking to Southampton
Yeovil to Exeter

EASTERN MAIN LINES
Ely to Kings Lynn
Fenchurch Street to Barking
Ipswich to Saxmundham
Liverpool Street to Ilford

WESTERN MAIN LINES
Ealing to Slough
Exeter to Newton Abbot
Newton Abbot to Plymouth
Paddington to Ealing
Plymouth to St. Austell
Slough to Newbury

COUNTRY RAILWAY ROUTES
Andover to Southampton
Bath Green Park to Bristol
Bath to Evercreech Junction
Bournemouth to Evercreech Jn.
Cheltenham to Andover
Croydon to East Grinstead
Didcot to Winchester
East Kent Light Railway
Fareham to Salisbury
Frome to Bristol
Guildford to Redhill
Reading to Basingstoke
Reading to Guildford
Redhill to Ashford
Salisbury to Westbury
Stratford upon Avon to Cheltenham
Strood to Paddock Wood
Taunton to Barnstaple
Wenford Bridge to Fowey
Westbury to Bath
Woking to Alton
Yeovil to Dorchester

GREAT RAILWAY ERAS
Ashford from Steam to Eurostar
Clapham Junction 50 years of change
Festiniog in the Fifties
Festiniog in the Sixties
Isle of Wight Lines 50 years of change
Railways to Victory 1944-46
SECR Centenary album
Talyllyn 50 years of change
Yeovil 50 years of change

LONDON SUBURBAN RAILWAYS
Caterham and Tattenham Corner
Charing Cross to Dartford
Clapham Jn. to Beckenham Jn.
Crystal Palace (HL) & Catford Loop
East London Line
Finsbury Park to Alexandra Palace
Kingston and Hounslow Loops
Lewisham to Dartford
Lines around Wimbledon
London Bridge to Addiscombe
Mitcham Junction Lines
North London Line
South London Line
West Croydon to Epsom
West London Line

London Suburban Railway continued .....
Willesden Junction to Richmond
Wimbledon to Beckenham
Wimbledon to Epsom

STEAMING THROUGH
Steaming through Cornwall
Steaming through the Isle of Wight
Steaming through Kent
Steaming through West Hants
Steaming through West Sussex

TRAMWAY CLASSICS
Aldgate & Stepney Tramways
Barnet & Finchley Tramways
Bath Tramways
Bournemouth & Poole Tramways
Brighton's Tramways
Burton & Ashby Tramways
Camberwell & W.Norwood Tramways
Clapham & Streatham Tramways
Croydon's Tramways
Dover's Tramways
East Ham & West Ham Tramways
Edgware and Willesden Tramways
Eltham & Woolwich Tramways
Embankment & Waterloo Tramways
Enfield & Wood Green Tramways
Exeter & Taunton Tramways
Greenwich & Dartford Tramways
Hammersmith & Hounslow Tramways
Hampstead & Highgate Tramways
Hastings Tramways
Holborn & Finsbury Tramways
Ilford & Barking Tramways
Kingston & Wimbledon Tramways
Lewisham & Catford Tramways
Liverpool Tramways 1. Eastern Routes
Liverpool Tramways 2. Southern Routes
Liverpool Tramways 3. Northern Routes
Maidstone & Chatham Tramways
Margate to Ramsgate
North Kent Tramways
Norwich Tramways
Portsmouth's Tramways
Reading Tramways
Seaton & Eastbourne Tramways
Shepherds Bush & Uxbridge Tramways
Southampton Tramways
Southend-on-sea Tramways
Southwark & Deptford Tramways
Stamford Hill Tramways
Twickenham & Kingston Tramways
Victoria & Lambeth Tramways
Waltham Cross & Edmonton Tramways
Walthamstow & Leyton Tramways
Wandsworth & Battersea Tramways

TROLLEYBUS CLASSICS
Croydon Trolleybuses
Bournemouth Trolleybuses
Hastings Trolleybuses
Maidstone Trolleybuses
Reading Trolleybuses
Woolwich & Dartford Trolleybuses

WATERWAY ALBUMS
Kent and East Sussex Waterways
London to Portsmouth Waterway
Surrey Waterways
West Sussex Waterways

MILITARY BOOKS
Battle over Portsmouth
Battle over Sussex 1940
Bombers over Sussex 1943-45
Bognor at War
Military Defence of West Sussex
Military Signals from the South Coast
Secret Sussex Resistance
Surrey Home Guard
Sussex Home Guard

OTHER RAILWAY BOOKS
Garraway Father & Son
Index to all Middleton Press stations
Industrial Railways of the South-East
South Eastern & Chatham Railways
London Chatham & Dover Railway
War on the Line (SR 1939-45)